OUR LADY
OF WISDOM

*Memling—Detail from the Diptych
of Martin van Nieuwenhove*

OUR LADY
OF WISDOM

by Maurice Zundel

New York

Sheed & Ward

1940

35601

NIHIL OBSTAT
  ARTHUR J. SCANLAN, S.T.D.,
    Censor Librorum

IMPRIMATUR
  ✠ FRANCIS J. SPELLMAN, D.D.,
    Archbishop, New York

New York, August 2, 1940.

CONTENTS

v

ILLUSTRATIONS

PROLOGUE

THE water of Jacob's well seems to have little enough connection with eternal life. Yet Jesus used it as the starting point for the instruction of the woman of Samaria.

Man has roots in flesh; you can elevate him only if you take as starting point of your effort something in which he finds the tang of reality.

This point is different for each man, but it must always be at the heart of his life.

Volumes of general arguments, be they ever so valid, remain without effect; you have to find the word which touches the living reality in him.

The world is a parable, every reality looks towards God; every one of our needs is the repercussion of our one single need for God who is the one thing necessary.

One can begin anywhere, provided that one touches life at that point.

No matter how you go about it, there is no flower where there are no roots.

The language of religion—apart from the sacred liturgy in which the soul is always filled full measure and running over—has too often become mortally wearisome, because an illusory angelism has left it bloodless. Words have taken on the faded look of confraternity ribbons passed on from mother to daughter. Words have lost their sap—yet these same words came forth from the Word of Life as reflected in the divine Thought of which all things are the expression.

They must be given back all their power of suggestion by the reawakening of all their spiritual vibrations, all their vital resonances. They will go straight to the soul—if they are real. Their message directly stated will develop by its own power in the recollection of the spirit, like the seed of the parable growing in silence. The soul's meeting with truth will have the shock of a discovery. Only on this condition, indeed, do the truths of faith become nourishment and not merely impediments cumbering the mind.

Our Lord constantly had recourse to this mode of starting from living experience—evoking a familiar scene, letting the spiritual truth of which it was the sensible analogue be glimpsed through it— as it were suggesting the fundamental note by its harmonic. His method was always to open a way for living experience, never to turn his back upon it.

No one would choose to give up the reality for the shadow. Men will never loosen their grip upon such reality as they hold unless they see, in the spiritual acceptance of the things the gospel proposes, the true fulfilment of all reality.

Every creature is secretly worked upon by grace. If at times it resists so fiercely, it is because it is not sure of the things it seems to possess. A mysterious ill-ease makes it feel how precariously it holds them.

Never tell it that any of the things dear to it will be taken away: if you do, it will simply withdraw within its threatened domain, rise in revolt against the assault from without, stand rigid in the defense of its outraged autonomy.

Rather make it see that its hold upon what it has held so precariously will be all the firmer, that all its vital powers cry out for a fulfilment beyond expression, that if it must yield it is through love, and that its yielding is to another who is more interior to it than its own being—and who loves it.

Once this point is reached, resistance ceases and the soul begins to enter into that divine poverty which is the recurring theme of the pages that follow. We shall see how this divine poverty belongs to the *interiority* which is the quality of a life genuinely spiritual—or rather how it is identical with it at every degree of perfection—whereas the spirit of possession coincides with the *exteriority* of the being, precipitating its fall into the unreal.

In this light the Blessed Virgin will be seen as

the fullest realisation, in the created order, of interiority of life in poverty according to the spirit.

How indeed could we do justice to her admirable title Seat of Wisdom, which is the subject of this book, save by showing Jesus in Mary, in the ordination of her whole virginal being to the Word which is the life and the light of men.

I

LOVE CRUCIFIED

THE Gospel begins with a tragedy of love, St. Matthew gives us a glimpse into its depths:

Now the generation of Christ was in this wise. When as his mother Mary was espoused to Joseph, before they came together she was found with child, of the Holy Ghost. Whereupon Joseph her husband, being a just man, and not willing publicly to expose her, was minded to put her away privately.

But while he thought on these things, behold the Angel of the Lord appeared to him in his sleep saying: Joseph, son of David, fear not to take unto thee Mary thy wife. For that which is conceived in her is of the Holy Ghost.

And she shall bring forth a son: and thou shalt call his name Jesus. For he shall save his people from their sins. . . .

And Joseph rising up from sleep, did as the Angel of the Lord had commanded him, and took unto him his wife. (Matt. 1, 18-24)

There is not a word too many or too few. In one movement we are brought to the heart of the Mystery: just so it had suddenly confronted Joseph. But we know what the issue was, and Joseph at that time did not.

He loved Mary. From the first moment of their first meeting he had felt that she was unique and that God was entrusting her to him. Was he now called upon to sacrifice her as Abraham had had to steel himself to the immolation of Isaac?

The wound in his heart was immeasurable. The plain fact was there. No denial, no tenderness could alter it. Her very innocence made his anguish more poignant. Another must be guilty, who should take the responsibility for what he had done.

Joseph could not speak of it to her since she had chosen to be silent. Any word would have been an outrage. Silence, his silence, should give him back his liberty for it attested his utter confidence in her.

Thus he came to his decision. And he slept the sleep that relaxes the body but not the soul's pain.

Only if we could concentrate in one heart all the admiration, devotion, fervour that Christian souls were to feel through all generations towards Mary could we form any idea of the love she must have inspired in Joseph, could we divine the immensity of the drama being acted in that hour.

What Dante sang of Beatrice, Joseph could have said in the richest fullness of meaning:

> *Vede perfettamente onne salute*
> *chi la mia donna tra le donne vede*

> He sees perfectly all salvation
> Who sees my Lady among women[1]

More than any other he felt that human nature was ennobled by her.[2] If he had dared to enter into the espousal, it was to guard the treasure—the treasure which now seemed irremediably lost.

The thought that by this marriage, which their first glance had ratified as an exchange of virginities, he had not been able to prevent a violation that was also a sacrilege, pierced his heart like a sword and sleep could not quiet the pain.

Meanwhile Mary watched in prayer, suffering in his suffering, living all the agony that her sealed lips could not abate in him.

[1] *Vita Nuova*, Son. XVI.
[2] Tu se'colei, che l'umana natura
Nobilitasti, sì, che'l suo Fattore
Non disdegnò di farsi sua fattura
                    (Dante, *Div. Com.* canto XXXIII)

The yes that bound her soul to Joseph's was all the more irrevocable in that it engaged her fidelity to God, who was the strong foundation of their union.

She had realised that a man of that quality would associate himself with the strange vow that consecrated her to God, would stand between her and the importunity of relations and the demands of custom.

Now that God had willed this miraculous blossoming of her maternity, so that she could not remain alone without raising a host of infamous rumours, was he to be taken from her?

As a virgin, she had consented to marriage, must she renounce marriage as a mother?

It was not, we may imagine, the disgrace she feared, but the wounds that insolence can deal to silence and the brutal invasion of her soul's deepest secrets.

She did not ask to know what the issue should be of a situation into which supreme obedience alone had brought her. She asked only that he should be spared.

It was then that the Angel intervened:

Joseph—he touches him lightly as a sleeping child—*Son of David*—heir of the promise which

shall be fulfilled in you—*fear not to take Mary*—
whose name breathes the freshness and the joy of
all the dawns—*thy wife*—the title which has made
her for ever yours in the sight of God—*for that
which is concerned in her*—thus the jubilation of all
the Christmas days to come resounds first in you—
is of the Holy Spirit—who is the eternity of love in
the eternity of being.[1]

And he took her to him.

It is impossible to conceive a more radical opposition to the spirit of possession which transforms so
many passions into enslavements, when two beings
fall under the intoxication of the absolute empire
each exercises over the other, when each sees the
other as the one thing necessary—thus promoting
each other to the rank of God, and each savouring
the adoration which attests his glory as last end.
In truth the illusion of adoration conceals a monstrous ego-centrism, which only clutches the more
avidly for talking the language of giving, and which
finds in the enchantment of the senses the magic
source of its ardour—until the day comes when the
eyes are opened to see what is really there, no God
but a poor shrunken human thing, seen in harsh

[1] This commentary is irresistibly suggested by the melody given in
the Vatican edition, to the text of communion for the Feast of St.
Joseph, March 19.

reality for what it is, incapable of stimulating or satisfying.

It happens not infrequently that, in the resentment at having been duped, the emotion that thought it was love turns to a hatred which proves that the original impulse towards the other was only the swollen projection of an ego, quickened by the sap of altruism, but egoism still.

It would, of course, be cruelly unjust were we to fail to see how much of sincerity and nobility and beauty there can be in the complexity of a profound passion in which, even if egocentrism is dominant, there still abides some element of altruism to reflect the divine poverty of love. But it would be no less unjust were we to fail to see the cosmic fatality with which passion often blazes up under the impulsion of the *élan vital* by which the species seeks to ensure its survival, or the torment brought to many by this insurgence of an instinct which submerges reason and all nobility without bringing them the least ray of light upon its nature, its origin and its end.

Is there, indeed, a more convincing sign of a primordial fall of man than this disastrous deviation in man of an instinct which is fundamentally nothing but the marvellous call of life?

That this instinct can so often break out in absolute unawareness of its fundamental reason, or what is worse, in the deliberate exclusion of the new life to whose production it is ordered; that the ecstasy which should be a creative ecstasy, the magnificent orchestration of an utter giving, the jubilation of two altruisms reaching out to the new being which is the fruit of their love, should be reduced to the mysterious[1] turbulence of a lightless union of two bodies tormented that they must remain two, since there is no communion of souls; surely all this is the most tragic evidence of a life grown exterior to itself, an activity no longer rooted in reality.

What a curious being is man, ceaselessly troubled by the thirst for the divine, and trying to appease his torment by divinising his body and making an absolute of a physical thrill—until the day when, in the silence of his listening soul, he meets the subsistent

[1] The whole problem here is to place the mystery. We feel that there is a mystery and that it is infinite. But what is it? It is only if we play with the surface of it that we lose our balance and are in peril of being destroyed by it. By going direct to the heart of it, ceasing to remain exterior to it, we come to see its true face and impure phantoms are dispersed. We can but deplore the lack of honesty generally displayed in the training of the creative faculties—indeed the systematic deformation to which they are subjected—in that all the attention of the young is centered upon possible sins, and they are not shown the call to holiness contained in this incredible power which God's trust has confided to them—the power to co-operate with him in the coming into existence of immortal souls, a power which makes the human body the tabernacle of life.

altruism of love itself, in which being and giving are one.

Then in truth he realises the essential impurity of possession and the folly of seeking to enclose within the limits of his ego a being not to be satisfied save by the light from heaven.

"So act," says Kant, "as to treat all humanity, whether in your own person or in others, as an end and never as a means." This must be understood of an immediate ordination of the soul to God, of such sort that it cannot attain its own fulfilment unless it loses itself in the abysses of eternal charity and participates in the infinite impulse of the divine altruism.

Clearly then a man and a woman—alike called to this divine fulfilment—can give themselves irrevocably to each other only in God and for God: becoming for each other as it were sacraments[1] of the Infinite, sacraments of the love which must unite them ever more perfectly to God, in an even more rigorous yielding up of their own selves:

Husbands, love your wives, as Christ also loved the church and delivered himself up for it: that he might sanctify it, cleansing it by the laver of water

[1] I here give the word "sacrament" the analogical meaning of a sensible reality which represents and in some manner communicates the Divine.

in the word of life. That he might present it to him-self a glorious church, not having spot or wrinkle, or any such thing, but that it should be holy and without blemish. (Eph. v. 25-27)

And

Let women be subject to their husbands, as to the Lord: because the husband is the head of the wife: as Christ is the head of the Church. He is the saviour of the [mystical] *body.* (Eph. v. 23)

If marriage is called to this height, if it is *in Christ* the sacrament which represents and in a certain manner accomplishes the mystery of the church, it is no matter for surprise that the union of two Chris-tians should be in the full stream of the supernatural life, under the primacy of divine Charity, whose in-effable altruism it symbolises in the flesh and con-firms in the spirit.[1]

Clearly we must expect to see marriage, obedient to the movement of grace, tend toward that virginity of heart which flowers in a flesh that has become as though interior to spirit—so that one thinks not of the soul as in the body but of the body as in the soul.

In fact, one does see marriages in which husband and wife limit their relations strictly to what life

[1] *Summa Theologica* I^a II^{ae}, q.34, art. 1; II^a II^{ae}, q.153, a.2; *Sup,* q.41, a.4.

itself requires for its continuation,[1] bending their whole purpose to the propagation of new life, in the sole design of offering to God a new temple for the habitation of His Spirit.

Surely we can hope that an ever wider recourse to the sources of the mystical life will direct Christian feeling ever more closely to the ideal represented at its highest by the marriage of Mary and Joseph: so that, in the light of the Wisdom which reconciles extremes by impressing upon all aspects of being the God-centredness of charity, conjugal love itself will become the guardian of virginity, bringing to life a tenderness wholly of God, in God and for God.

Already for us it is a marvellous illumination to realize that the division of the sexes consecrates the man and the woman to the child, sealing in their flesh the first elements of its corporeal life, and thus in their very bodies prefiguring the profound altruism that is expressed in fatherhood and motherhood. And when the vital impulse threatens to darken reason, it is a marvellous refuge to purify its urge in the consideration of the being to which nature has ordained it. Our deep-lying disturbance

[1] Not through any contempt of the flesh, but in the luminous consciousness of its fundamental ordination to life—which implies that one loves the body with a very great charity and wills its supreme fulfilment in intimate association with the life of the spirit.

Bas-relief from Chartres

is calmed as the mystery that has troubled us takes upon itself the face of a child.

It is the child that is the fundamental reason for the instinct that tears at us, the child with the high dignity of his spiritual soul, with the capacity for God which is in him—as in those who have engendered him—a demand for holiness.

As this image grows in strength, it can and does happen that the flesh is calmed, submits more readily to the ordering of the spirit, and feels a pure joy in being in some manner associated with the ever active fecundity of the spirit, which propagates the divine life in the communion of saints.

Now if this reference to the child that may be born and the thought of the sanctuary of Divinity that his soul may be can work so powerfully upon us, what must have been the power of the feeling wrought in Mary and Joseph by the real presence of the Child who was God?

Mary, gathering in her heart all the expectation of Israel, had yet chosen to remain a virgin that her whole being might be one upward surge of love to God.

If she had consented to the tenderness of Joseph, it was that she had either discovered or originated the same design in him. God was to be the sole inter-

change of a marriage which should consist solely "in
the indivisible union of souls."[1]

When Mary became miraculously the Mother of
the Saviour, this undertaking received the most ineffable consecration. Her maternity was the supreme
fulfilment of her virginity, the divine flower of her
giving, the crowning of that love which from the
first moment took her utterly out of her own possession, the lily of poverty.

In taking Mary to his home in the fulfilment of
the ceremony which rendered their marriage defini-
tive, Joseph participated in the maternity of his
spouse in the measure in which he was vowed to her
virginity. That is to say that he was entirely consecrated to it and that it accomplished his own fecundity, as it did Mary's, in that marvellous fruit which
was the work of the Holy Spirit.

Thus it was that she could later say with the most
moving tenderness and the most exquisite humility:
"Thy father and I have sought thee sorrowing"
(Lk. ii. 48).

Jesus was truly the issue of their marriage, their
virginity was fruitful, their flesh exultant and at
peace, in the super-eminent realisation of the life-
bearing impulse. And as the bond that united them

[1] *Summa Theologica* III[a], q.29, a.2.

was the divine Person of their Child, their marriage at once holy and eternal, combining in a unique degree all elements of the perfect union—*fides, proles, sacramentum,* fruitfulness, fidelity, indissolubility.

Nor must we forget that to Mary all these titles belong with incontestable primacy: Joseph's virginity was a reflection of her own, his fatherhood was a consequence of her motherhood, and it was by uniting him for ever to Mary that the presence of Jesus confirmed him in grace and established him in that eminent holiness whose rays are over all the Church.

Yet this primacy of Mary did not reverse the natural order which made Joseph the head of the Holy Family. As Jesus obeyed them both, so Mary was lovingly subject to Joseph with that magnanimous humility which makes obedience love's attention to Love.

As with all the mysteries which involve Mary, her marriage was wholly contained in that "be it done unto me according to thy word," which ruled all the movements of her soul according to the demand of the gift of Wisdom, by which she was wholly yielded up to the eternal Wisdom who was

His Father's only Son and hers—like the divine song of her poverty in the infinite transparence of a shadowless love.

Eructavit cor meum verbum bonum
My heart hath uttered a good word. (Ps. xliv. 2)

Christian husbands and wives, whose love must at times pass through periods of anguished darkness not unlike the Dark Nights of the mystical union, must not forget that the marriage of the Virgin was begun under the sign of sorrow.

She who was in ineffable fullness Wife and Mother will teach them to seek, in setting God ever more perfectly as the centre of all their aims and affections, the solution of the problems that torment them; and she will teach them that wisdom, which is the fruit of a love totally stripped of self, all poverty of spirit, like that which makes of her the

Sedes Sapientiae et Mater pulchrae Dilectionis
Seat of Wisdom
and Mother of Beautiful Love.

II

The Woman Who Was Poor

ONCE the sense of the spiritual life is dimmed, the individual person is sacrificed to collective myths.

For if the supreme Good does not dwell within us as the object with which we must be ever more closely united, if all human activities do not receive their unity from a common ordination to the life within us, then we have no other resource, if we would prevent the scattering of our forces and secure to ourselves some sort of immortality, save the rigorous cohesion and the impersonal continuity of the group or tradition.

Certain men emerge in whom the myth—of group or tradition—seems to be incarnate, for it acts only on condition of being strongly seized by a consciousness which expresses it. It is, then, in the hands of these men that all men's rights lie. Other men participate only in so far as these men judge compatible with the requirements of the myth.

We have no right to think that bad faith, pride or ambition alone presides over this allotment of rights.[1] When the value of the *person* is not known, there is no other means of giving a meaning to life. The myth is necessarily enthroned as the dynamic personification of ends that transcend the individual. In all this there is a beginning of altruism that we must not despise. The myth may include things good and worthy of respect. The error is in making it a God.

If there is an Absolute—as every scale of values implies that there is—it is folly to expect to find anything of it in man save a deep-lying need and a destructive absence, so long as life has man for its centre. Multitudes all living together, or following generation by generation, cannot alter that truth. They are still only men.

We must not lose sight of these considerations

[1] We may see in Plato's *Republic*, especially in Book V, with what fervent obstinacy a great mind is capable of inculcating monstrous things when it lets itself be guided by an entirely abstract view of man and his good. The way Aristotle speaks of "individuals destined by nature to slavery" or of the inferiority of virtue in women in Book I of the *Politics*; the counsels he gives, on the lines of Plato, on birth control and the suppression of deformed children in Book IV, lead us to think that "the Greek miracle," whose art gives us such perfect examples, had at its heart a hidden cry for a redemption which should give to life the divine balance which sanctity alone can reveal as sanctity alone can bring it to pass.

in forming a clear view of the place of woman in antiquity.

If according to the laws which prevailed in Rome or Athens, she was always a minor, if "in death as in life she counted only as a member of her husband,"[1] it was because the permanence of the family, symbolised by the flame of the hearth and sustained by the worship of the ancestors, was the supreme law of domestic life. But this continuity could be assured only by women, hence it was their lot to enter by marriage the family of others. Thus the man was master, not so much in his own name as in the name of the line of which he was for the time being the head.

This situation—which by no means excluded marital love—grew slacker with the centuries, at least for free women, in proportion as belief weakened and the solidarity of the family became less assured.

But it would seem that the principle upon which it was based had never been formally repudiated until womanhood showed itself for what it truly was in the maternity of Mary.

Quae est ista quae ascendit sicut aurora consurgens
Pulchra ut luna, electa ut sol,

[1] Fustel de Coulanges, *La Cité antique*, p. 94.

Terribilis ut castrorum acies ordinata?

*Who is she that cometh forth as the morning ris-
ing, fair as the moon, bright as the sun, terrible as an
army set in array?* (Cant. vi. 9)

Humanity turned again toward its source, or
rather its source came to it. We were to learn what
that life contains which has been handed on from
generation to generation since the beginning of
men, and which is genuinely lived by so small a
number—as if men were content blindly to transmit
its richness, without bothering their heads as to its
nature and significance:

Behold the man comes who is born of the Spirit.

"Because," says the Seraphic Doctor, "the love of
God burned in the heart of the Virgin in a unique
manner in her flesh He accomplished miracles."[1]

"It is no small thing for the saints," says the
Angelic Doctor, "to have the amount of grace that
suffices to sanctify their souls; but the soul of the
Blessed Virgin had grace in such abundance that it
overflowed from the soul upon her body, and in
such marvellous measure that she conceived in her
body the Son of God."[2]

[1] In III, D.4, a.1, q.1.
[2] *Expos. sup. salut. angel. inter opuscula,* ed. Mandonnet IV, p. 458.

It was neither of blood, nor of the flesh, nor of the will of man that the Child could be born who was to give "to all those that received him the power to be made the sons of God":

Behold the woman comes who was conceived by the Spirit.

Perhaps now it will be clear that a child is a capacity for God, and that if its origin is to be worthy of its end, then maternity is primarily a function of the spirit.

It will no longer be possible to be unaware that woman belongs to the eternal order of which the visible world is but a symbol, that she has a personal destiny and an infinite dignity, that all her glory is within.

Omnis gloria eius ab intus. (Ps. xliv. 14)

What a liberation and what a destiny, what light and what purity! A new vision is given to man in the realisation of woman as having a spiritual function, woman "so gentle seeming and so honourable that every tongue trembles and is silent, and no eye dare look upon her."[1]

Henceforward, if any ask what is the place of woman, the answer must be: In God.

[1] Cf. Dante *Vita nuova, Son.* XV.

From this point of view, there is no difference between man and woman; and as it is the supreme consideration, it must come before all others.

The hierarchy of function which exists under the authority of the father in a well ordered family in no way lessens the *personal* autonomy of the wife and mother. God Himself revealed and consecrated the dignity of her mind and her heart when he required Mary's consent to the Mystery of the Incarnation.

It is impossible to form a true idea of God unless it is grasped that he communicates being to creatures by His very presence.[1] And as His presence is identical with Himself, it is natural to wonder how God could become incarnate, if on the one hand He can suffer no change, and on the other hand He was already wholly present in man, as indeed in every creature.

Clearly there can be no question that God's Presence is God Himself, and that It is as total in every being as He is in Himself indivisible. But if God is always present with the creature, it is far from true that the creature is always present with God. The commonest attitude is all too well described in Augustine's burning avowal:

[1] *Summa Theol.*, 1ᵃ; q.8, a.1.

"Too late have I loved thee, beauty so ancient and so new. Too late have I loved thee. And lo! Thou wert within and I was without, and there I sought thee; and to those lovely things which thou hast made I rushed lacking all loveliness. Thou wert with me, and I was not with thee. And those things kept me far from thee which, if they were not in thee, would not have been."[1]

It was on the creature's part that there was something to change, not on God's.

St. Thomas expresses this with admirable force: "The mystery of the Incarnation was not accomplished in that God was withdrawn in any manner from the state in which He was from all eternity, but in that He united Himself in a new way to the creature, or rather it to Himself."[2]

Consider the great refusal of love which darkens

[1] The divine Presence, which is wholly spiritual and not to be confused with presence in space, is the more intimate as it is more intimately received. For each being it is proportional to the degree in which it is capable of responding to the divine action.

If it is free and can increase in its adhesion (as in its refusal) the divine Presence is susceptible of variation in the same measure, not of course in itself but in the subject which receives its influx. The Presence we are here discussing, that to which man owes his supernatural being, is precisely of such sort that it cannot normally be without his consent. It can therefore vary with the degree of his consent.

This is not true of the action (or if you prefer the influence or the presence) to which we owe our physical existence, which is independent of our consent and cannot be more or less.

[2] *Summa Theol.*, III^a; q.1, a.1, ad 1.

the splendour of man's origin, the deviation of humanity in its head, the diversion of man toward self which shattered his unity by scattering all his powers, the pride which swings man from his true centre, takes him outside his own being, immerses him in matter by delivering him to all the assaults of the outer world and subjecting him to all the fatalities of matter.

To all this, Love, whose fullness is not diminished by our failure, was to oppose that new creation which is now accomplished in the womb of the Virgin—a Humanity all stripped of self and gravitating in the field of the Divinity, a Humanity which had its Self in God, a Humanity subsisting in the Word as the living sacrament of the eternal Mind,[1] the Sacred Humanity of our Lord Jesus Christ "who is over all things God blessed for ever." (Rom. ix. 5)

An infinite Altruism shines in the depths of the

[1] "Our Lord is therefore the Sacrament par excellence, which all the other sacraments represent and whence they all are derived; the purpose of the Eucharist in the Church Militant is to preserve for us in its substantial reality the sacrament of sacraments which is its Head" (Schwalm: *Le Christ d'après St. Thomas*).

This notion of sacrament is the key to Christian theology. The divine Reality which is the basis of the doctrine is communicated to us by signs in which the sacred Humanity of Christ energises. But the divine Reality itself while it is in the signs is infinitely above them, and this it is that we seek in an ineffable contact which it is the purpose of the sacraments to render ever more immediate and personal, through the pure translucence of their efficacy in which that Light is given which remains incomprehensible by any creature.

Godhead, in the circumincession of the Persons who are bound each to each in the subsistent *élan* which makes each as it were a living relation to the other two. And this infinite Altruism makes possible so radical a yielding up of self in the Humanity assumed, that every fibre of its being is a pure upward surge toward God.

The Word of God, light of light, subsistent image of the Father's face, now in the shadowless transparence of a soul and body all stripped of self expresses itself whole and entire and illumines the night of our darkness with the brightness of eternity.

This ineffable union of divine Poverty and human is as a substantial consecration which causes the realisation in Jesus of the crown and consummation of the aspiration of every mystical life—to have its self in God—the aspiration which gave Mary the only begotten Son of the Father to be her Son.

Now if Mary is, so to speak, the place of this confluence of Divine and human altruism, Divine and human poverty, if she is the sanctuary of this rite of consecration, obviously she could not remain outside it, with her whole being she must have been borne into the very depths of it. Before the Incarnation, she was already wholly God's: she was offered and given, she was poor, she waited. But she did not yet know with what plenitude the word of the Canticle was to be fulfilled in her:

> *Ego dilecto meo*
> *Et ad me conversio eius*
> *I to my beloved*
> *And his turning is towards me.* (Cant. vii. 10)

Certainly she knew the Scriptures by heart. She had grasped their secret movement, the Christward direction of every word, how the burning breath of the Spirit consumed all the taints and impurities of humanity in the human words to which God had entrusted His message. In Scripture she sought a Presence, she found a Person in whom all the hope of humanity rested. Her heart beat only to the cry:

That a Virgin should conceive and bear a Son. (Is. vii. 14)

It was never in her mind that this referred to her. Her gaze had one single direction and never wavered from it. Her gaze was utterly direct: she never saw herself at all.

When the Angel appeared and the first *Ave* sounded, she was puzzled as to what the message might mean and who the messenger might be. If he spoke truth, if he came from God, then his word could not contradict the design of virginity which God himself had inspired in her:

"How shall this be done, because I know not man?"

"The Holy Ghost shall come upon thee, and the Power of the most High shall overshadow thee."

(Luke i, 34-35)

Sure that it was God who called her, she uttered her consent in the word which had first on the lips of God called creation into being in wonderful dignity, and which now on her lips re-established it in dignity more wonderful—the word *fiat*, be it done.

"Behold the handmaid of the Lord,
Be it done unto me according to thy word."

She was the Mother of God.

She who knew the prophets so well knew what awaited her. The first notes of the *Stabat Mater* already sounded in her heart.

But she who had taken no account of herself ever was not likely to be concerned about herself now, in the very moment when all that had in any way survived of self was effaced in Him, when all her being was for ever immersed in His mystery so that henceforth she was nought save a living relation to Him. Supremely stripped of self, she could now only give herself eternally in the Child she had conceived of the Holy Spirit—not as the glorified image of herself but as the splendour of the Father's glory shining through the transparence of her poverty.

Her very motherhood consummated her yielding up of all that was hers. In a unique sense she was the Woman who was Poor.

Cum essem parvula placui altissimo,
Et de meis visceribus genui Deum et hominem.
As I was small, I pleased the most High
And of my womb I bore Him who is God and man.

When the Angel was gone, she thought of those who waited in the expectation of the Life which was coming through her. She rose and went to Elizabeth to inaugurate that mission which she was never to cease to accomplish, bearing Christ in her and arousing from their night his children seated in the shadow of death as she sets echoing in their heart the cry which preludes the Gospel in the Liturgy called that of St. John Chrysostom:

Sophia: orthói

Wisdom: arise

III

Holy Silence

I HAVE dreamed of building a church to Silence as Sancta Sophia is dedicated to Wisdom. It will be called Hágia Sigê, and it will never be anything but a dream.

It will be separated from the street by a cloister, and in the midst of the cloister will be the peaceful greenness of a lawn. Winding paths, on which our footsteps raise no echo, lead to doors that open and close silently.

Deep carpets absorb the sound of steps within the church. Quiet hangings stir faintly on the walls of the apse in the light of the lamps.

In the raised sanctuary, the altar is a table of alabaster, all but translucent from a light within. The tabernacle is of onyx, similarly but more intensely translucent.

The eyes turn naturally to it and remain fixed upon it. The whole atmosphere absorbs you in the one Being necessary.

The Mass proceeds there as the chant of silence. There is no sound. The vestments spiritualise the body of the priest, the gestures are lived, the voices interior. An invisible presence is the air that all souls breathe.

Made actual in the mystic oblation, the Cross arises to enfold them all in its life-giving embrace, and the Host comes to them as a divine ferment.

The sacred Action over, each one departs, lost in God, to bear to his brethren a ray of God's face, in the silence of a life where there is no echo save of God's Word.

That is my dream of Hágia Sigê, the basilica of silence.

It is in the liturgy that souls must learn to listen, so that the unique Word in which is all truth may be uttered in them.

To listen!—the highest, rarest, most necessary action.

Words are always running ahead of thought, imposing on thought the burden of their materiality, all that is in them of error and passion, all their garnishing of irrational impulses and collective suggestions. We judge before we have examined, take sides before we know. We have not the art of waiting, of remaining open, while the problem is allowed to ripen in the clear air of the unhurried mind. And with our own limits we proceed to find others. In extreme cases, crowds beyond numbering, whole peoples, are the victims of a pseudo-idea, erected into an idol by some vibrant formula whose endless repetition sets up in the individual's nervous system reflexes which react automatically, and explosively, at the first appeal.

And after all, once spiritual values cease to be preponderant, the only way to avoid anarchy is to draw from the instincts of the mob that which shall subject the mob under the guise of expressing its will: one can but manage public opinion so as to make it demand what its leaders want.

I do not say that all is necessarily bad in what is thus suggested to the crowd, but what contempt for man there is in this prostitution of mind, what an ignoring of spirit in this animal magnetism of words.

Words no longer convey the light of thought; exterior to true humanity, made of dynamic images and charged solely with power to impel, they tend only to unchain action by sweeping aside all hesitation of conscience, all resistance of free-will.

It is not enough to produce the same automatic gesture from bodies—outstretched arm or clenched fist; they want to produce in minds the rigidity of the same automatic judgment.

We know how infallibly this tendency prevails under all regimes and in all parties, once the spirit loses its primacy and as a consequence the dignity of the person is lost in the oppression of the individual under the tyranny of the mass.

And the slavery is all the more deep-rooted the more spontaneously it is accepted, is the more irremediable in proportion to the number of true ideas pressed into the task of dragging humanity towards an inhuman goal.

Silence alone reveals the depths of life. That is why thinkers need it even more than men of action. Thinkers it is who in the ordinary way guide men's minds to the sources. Unless they *listen*, let the light flow through them, turn from themselves, they cannot make "that jump over their shadow which would land them in the sunlight";[1] and truth will lose its own face and be seen with theirs, while they invest with the prestige of science the interpretations which their fundamental choice, their general attitude in the face of life, imposes upon their discoveries.

It would be a glorious thing if in every master, and still more in every parent, there were a reverence for the minds entrusted to him, no other aim

[1] Nietzsche *Zarathustra*.

Filippino Lippi—From the
Apparition to St. Bernard

save to establish contact between these minds and the light; so that the teacher effaces himself before the mystery of a contact which in each mind must be utterly personal.

A child, admittedly, needs to be formed, but by the development of his interior life primarily as he learns to listen to the Master teaching him from within his being. We should not scold him and thereby irritate a nervous system already over-excited; we should not render him still more ex-terior to his own soul than he is already. Rather the whole of our effort should be to bring him back to the life deep within him, helping him to the awareness of the divine Presence by the irradiation of silence: for silence is the essential factor of all genuine education. The point is not to substitute oneself for the child or make him as like oneself as possible, but to bring him to his interior guide before whom one's own self should be utterly effaced.

Consider now the care that is imposed upon theo-logians and spiritual directors, whose proper task is to expound the mysteries of God and proportion souls to their measure. Immeasurable delicacy of touch is necessary and profound humility, filial fear and prostration before that Truth which is the very life of God in the generation of His Word. There must be an abiding awareness of the limits of speech and the powerlessness of words, a thirst for the Reality beyond towards which words draw us, for all the unsayable that we glimpse in them, for the depths, masked to us by their veils, where lies "the mighty abyss of the Godhead."[1]

It would be a betrayal of trust to forget, even for an instant, the tendency faith has to go beyond itself towards that initial knowledge in which revealed truths are no longer separately seen in their customary statement: for they are no longer dispersed in verbal formulas but brought together in the unique focus of the eternal Light; they are perceived in God, in the very life that they enunciate and of which they are some beginning in us; they have grown "sensible to the heart" by the Charity which sets us *within* that Life, yet without rending the veil which seals it from our eyes.

Each of these truths, indeed, takes the inflection of the loved Being, like a shared secret in which the soul savours the Presence which establishes a mysterious relation—akin to the circuminsession of the Trinity—between all revealed truths.

In this light of love, all is seized "in the very gift

[1] Cf. John of Saint-Thomas *Les dons du Saint-Esprit*, translated by Raïssa Maritain, pp. 141-3, 186, 187.

God makes of Himself, giving Himself to us by His spirit and His will as if He were bringing us His heart."[1] And it is this light which gives the theologian that instinct for the Divine which is indispensable for the perfection of his science.

In this affective wisdom, the theologian sometimes arrives at such a simplicity of gaze, that the division into concepts seems utterly derisory, the all-sufficingness of light suffers no apprehension as of distinct truths, and his knowledge is akin to the simple mode of the knowledge of God Himself.

It is then that he can speak of that "sublime ignorance which is attained by virtue of a union beyond comprehension"[2]—not because he is lost in something vague and incoherent, but because he has become aware of a Reality so dazzling that anything that belongs to the human mode of knowing is seen to be powerless.

"At this point you will ask me," says the author of *The Cloud of Unknowing*, "how I can think of God and what He is, and to this question I can make only one reply: 'I know nothing of it.'"

It is in the same sense that St. Thomas ceased the writing of the *Summa* with an avowal of impotence: "I can no more; all that I have written, in com-

---

[1] John of Saint-Thomas, *ibid.*, p. 138.
[2] Dionysius, *De Divinis Nominibus*.

parison with what I have seen, seems to me no better than straw."

The Doctor and the Mystic were too closely identified in him for the Doctor to be able to linger in discourse once the Mystic had transcended it. The *Summa* could not be completed save "by that leap into sunlight," in the exposition of the Canticle wherein the Spirit celebrates the mystical marriage of the soul with God.

It is in this perspective that we must read it, making our own way towards the theology which rather "experiences divine things" than learns them.

It is toward this "I know not," that beginners must be directed: such a sense of ultimate ineffableness must be communicated to them as will prevent them applying too material a logic to the things of God; they must be given a thirst for that Reality beyond, which no distinct apprehension can seize here below, in order that their theology may tend humbly towards infused contemplation as its crown and consummation; they must be helped to hear the mystical resonances of a doctrine which bears upon the innermost life of God, a doctrine therefore in which one makes no progress save by losing oneself in Him.

Spiritual direction will naturally have the same tendency as theological training: it sees the soul in

the light of the divine mystery which is being accomplished in it; it knows with what reverence God
disposes of it,[1] "for one can scarcely touch it but it
bleeds;"[2] and the director can have no other aim but
to strip it of all sense of ownership of itself in order
that it may be even more utterly in the hand of the
Holy Spirit. Thus the director effaces himself, as a
servant of the interior life, before the beloved Guest
who is secretly leading it towards Himself.

Direction, therefore, like theology requires poverty of spirit, the silence which *listens* in order to
welcome the truth within itself as it would welcome
a person.

For truth *is* a person, a divine Person, the only-
begotten Son who is in the bosom of the Father: the
Silent Word.

Silent, because totally interior[3] to its Principle and
expressing Him alone in a fundamental self-giving—
a note utterly pure, the translucid echo of a virginal

[1] *Wisdom* XII, 18. Cf. The offertory of St. Genevieve

Stetit Genovefa juxta thronum Dei
Orans pro salute languentis populi,
Cum Matre Domini Virgine Maria:
Quas Deus audivit cum reverentia.

Genevieve stood before the throne of God, praying for the salvation of
the people who were falling away, with the Virgin Mary, mother of the
Lord: and God heard them with reverence.

[2] *John of St. Thomas, op. cit.,* p. 113.

[3] All discord wounds the ear like the clash of sounds whose vibrations remain exterior, out of relation, one to another. When the vibrations are complementary and merge together we have the impression
of harmony and of silence.

generation, an ecstasy of light that hymns light, a living harmony with no discord, a subsistent music wherein the whole being is but the one cry: Abba, Father!

"But I have called you friends: because all things whatsoever I have heard of my Father, I have made known to you" (John xv. 15). For "the things I have heard of him, these same I speak in the world" (John viii. 26).

Thus the eternal Speech is the Word that listens, the silent Word.

And Mary was a disciple of the Word. She kept in her heart all the words of her Son (Luke ii. 51). She listened, adhered, gave herself, was utterly immersed in the abyss of His being:

> *Let thy voice sound in my ears:*
> *for thy voice is sweet and thy face comely.*
> (Cant. ii. 14)

Every fibre of her being vibrated with that appeal whereby her life was given wholly as a listening to the unique Truth: Jesus, Jesus, Jesus!

Her flesh was the cradle of the eternal Word springing from the "sealed fountain" of her soul;

her Magnificat is the exultation of the Word in the deepest places of her heart:

Dum medium silentium tenerent omnia . . .
While all things held the depth of silence and the night was at the midmost of her course, Thy almighty Word, O Lord, came down from heaven, from its royal throne.[1]

Is not Mary that royal throne, since all her powers resound with the mysteries that are cried forth in the silence of God,[2] since in the night of her unawareness of self she is all lost in the divine brightness of her Child?

She says nothing of herself, does nothing of herself, intermingles nothing of herself. By no idea, or image, or word is the Ineffable limited in her; and the splendour of divine Light meets in her no shadow.

She does not understand,[3] nor desire to understand, what the Infinite alone can comprehend in its fullness.

[1] Introit of Sunday within the Octave of Christmas. Cf. Wisdom XVIII, 14, 15.
[2] St. Ignatius of Antioch, Ep. xix. 1.
[3] "And they understood not the word that he spoke unto them" (Lk. ii. 50).

She offers her transparence as a pure window to the sun, and the Mystery of Jesus flames through her unhindered.

The rare occasions on which Mary appeared in the public life of the Saviour seem to be related only to show how rigorous was her self-effacement.[1]

We have no word of hers spoken to the Church after Her Son left the earth. The teaching she gave was infinitely more precious. While the apostles spoke, she by her silence led souls to the *Wisdom* whose mother she is.

It was within her heart that the first Christians felt the birth of that mysterious liberty wherein they rejoiced to know themselves as sons of the Father and brethren of Jesus.

She is the garden enclosed and the solitary place,

[1] As they likewise manifest the infinitely more rigorous self-efface-ment of the sacred Humanity of the Saviour in the Word which was His true Self. Thus when Jesus at Cana seems to refuse His Mother's request, He simply tells her that He undertakes nothing of Himself and that His meat is to do the will of His Father. Exactly as His doctrine is not His, so in the same sense His works are not His. His Humanity is "in the hand of the Holy Ghost, who gives it to the Word," as "the great sacrament of piety." It could not withdraw itself for an instant from the divine motion which regulates all the move-ments of its being without ceasing to be itself. "Mother, why be troubled, we are in the hand of the Father, we need but betake our-selves to Him." Mary understood him better than anyone, she united her obedience with His, and the miracle was the result of this two-fold submission. Cf. Bremond, *Histoire du sentiment religieux*, III, pp. 63, 84.

the nave all quiet and the lamp of recollection, the triumphal apse and the translucent altar.

She is the living tabernacle and the eternal altar of repose.

She is Hágia Sigê:

The Basilica of Silence

IV

STABAT MATER

WHAT will be the fate of the word—any word—
which issues from your lips and falls upon the ear
of those who hear you?

What shape will it take in their mind as it rico-
chets from the mysterious wave of the moving stream
of their thought?

We tend to assume that words in the same language have always the same sense for all who hear
them. Dictionaries give you strict definitions of their
meaning.

But what a difference of level in the reality signi-
fied to the intelligence. As a pebble bounds over the
mirror-like surface of a clear lake, making ever-
widening circles, but is swallowed up at once if the
surface is broken with waves, so the word you utter
can have repercussions without end in a transparent
mind, and die without echo in a soul deafened with
its own tumult.

Each one understands it according to what he is,

and interprets it in the light of his experience—in which is involved the whole mystery of his personality.

What reality can that personality accord to your word, save such as brings no wound to its own reality?

It has innumerable ways of escape from the reality it cannot bear, from refusal to listen to polite acquiescence.

Indeed it is all too possible to admire the structure of a towering system of ideas without the least intention of making one's own spiritual abode in it, to pay homage to the splendour of order while remaining disorderly oneself.

Anthropomorphism we know as the tendency to give a human form to objects of knowledge, to conceive them in our image. But it has not been sufficiently noted how widespread is this anthropomorphism in us, how almost incurable is our tendency to give every truth our own countenance.

To know we must be reborn: we must be wholly new and offer to the light a flawless transparence: we must be perfectly disinterested to let ourselves be acted upon by all the intelligible data of human experience: in fact *we must* be poor in spirit.

The finest culture of certain minds often remains

entirely sterile for lack of that preliminary denudation of self in them, that purity of heart which appeases the man of desires that is in every one of us and leaves us to be conquered only by the evidence of truth.

One is constantly startled at the impulsive character of their reactions, the support they give to the worst currents of opinion, their lack of respect for the human person when its owner is not in their camp.

But how can a thought obedient to its own movement possibly be universal, if one does not perceive the infinite value involved in all the activities of the mind, the element of divinity that is in the works of the noblest scholars from that species of consecration which is theirs, and which gives to research the character of a silent dialogue in which their primary rôle is to listen to truth.

For in every encounter with being, we invisibly confront the Word of God by whom all things were made.

There is no reason why man should sacrifice himself for truth, as so many searchers have done or felt bound in conscience to do, if truth were not more than man, if it did not transcend the order of things.

True intellectualism implies an exchange of life

which for the most part is felt rather than explicitly realised. One yields to a mysterious presence, one offers one's life that a Life may be expressed through it which is infinite. That is why research goes ever deeper and never reaches—nor even envisages—completion: for indeed it always bears the character of a *communion* of which no formula can be more than a provisional symbol.

Already, therefore, on the plane of scientific knowledge, there is the demand for purification,[1] failing which the dialogue can but turn into a duel, in which truth must succumb to the constraint forced upon it by the limitation of the seeker's mind.

[1] Unless regard is taken of the circuminsession of the intellectual life and the moral life and of the necessary rectification of the mind's vision by purity of heart, culture will turn to catastrophe. Ideas accumulated in the memory without having turned to light in the transparence of spirit will serve only to construct the monstrous edifice, after the image of man's desire, whose unbreakable framework of concepts will hold the whole being hopelessly captive. In the most favourable cases they will remain merely notions—in Newman's sense of the word notional—exterior to the mind in an illusory objectivity: for true objectivity can exist only in the purity of a gaze entirely detached from self and sensible only to the light of being (*mens obiiciens se lumini*).

It is clear today that the sciences common to all peoples who hold themselves for civilised do not in fact bind these peoples in a closer communion but are handled as explosives—the most abominable of all—in the conflicts that bring them into opposition.

A truly humanist—that is a truly human—education is bound indissolubly to that moral elevation which will make it a spiritual life. From this point of view, the chapel still to be found in the old colleges of Oxford and Cambridge remains at least an admirable symbol.

True knowing is a form of obedience.

Hence it is easy to see through what crucibles the spirit must pass to live by the divine Thought *as it is in itself*, and not simply capture the reflections of it in the universe.

Natural knowledge begins with that light of consciousness caused in us by the impact of the external world upon our sense structure. It progresses in the ever more perfect interiority of subject and object— the knower and the thing known.

It is our mind which brings to nature the active light which fertilises so to speak nature's latent intelligibility and so makes nature actually intelligible. Further our mind in some manner regulates the mysterious invasion of us by things in assimilating them according to the measure of its own maturity.

Natural knowledge is thus according to the measure of the man. Without deforming objects, he can leave them in a discreet half-light, postponing till later the task of investigating them more closely or leaving the task to others. In supernatural knowledge the light comes not from the mind but from above, infused in us by the spirit whose gaze is upon the profound mysteries of God. Therefore it is not within our power to regulate its movement. And, if we could, it would profit us nothing.

So we must pass from anthropomorphism—the tendency to see all things in our own likeness—to theomorphism—the aspiration to identify ourselves ever more perfectly with God: we must pass from the human mode of knowing to the divine. That this may be achieved, the initiative must be taken by God: and part of God's action is shown in the crucifying stages of the mystical *nights* in which man is little by little stripped of self until his identification with Christ is complete.

St. John of the Cross and St. Theresa have expressed, precisely and magnificently, the normal development of mystical experience.[1]

They have told of the terrible intensity of that light which exiles the creature from himself by cutting him off from his sense-activity, his intellect, even from God as He had till then been known.

They have described the suspension over the abyss, the utter isolation, the burning sense of unworthiness, the inexorable dark, the reduction to nothingness whose horror is past all saying and which seems to dislocate the soul in a fearful anathema. They have told of the ecstasies that seem to ravish the soul from the body, the sudden illuminations which bathe it in infinite light, the joy so

[1] See *The Mystical Doctrine of St. John of the Cross*, translated by Fr. Steuart S.J. (Sheed & Ward).

violent that it must bring death if God did not intervene to prevent that effect.

This initiation is not of course accompanied, in all souls that abandon themselves to the divine embrace, by all the phenomena and all the favours described in *The Interior Castle*. Many experience none of these mysterious visitations save the wholly interior action which preserves the secret of them, and thus do not clearly discern the stages they pass through in an obscurity which hides them from themselves. But the one thing rigorously necessary for all souls is that they should die to the spirit of possession that rivets them to self and become, in the spirit of poverty, wholly God's.

When the gift is consummated and the whole being utterly receptive to the divine mode of the transforming union, the body is so perfectly interior to the soul and the soul so perfectly interior to God, that contemplation is no longer the faintest difficulty. On the contrary, contemplation not only stirs to life in each an echo of itself, but also it finds in each the co-operation of a new urge. All the fibres of the being are but one voice hymning God. Creatures are no longer an obstacle: they enter the marvellous cycle in which their night sparkles like a procession of stars in a summer sky. They are no longer external but within us, all loved, all as brethren, each regaining its fullness of reality in the ray of ineffable love with which God loves it.

It is perfect joy in divine freedom, and the Canticle of the Sun is its eternal music.

The soul of course still remains capable of suffering, not now for itself, but as a victim of love for the salvation of others.

It is by this title alone that the Mother of the Creator knew the trials of the interior life. She had no need to be purified, for nothing in her opposed the least resistance to the accomplishment of the kingdom of God. She was "above the weakness of ecstasy," for in ecstasy is manifested the rigidity of a nature in which all is not wholly obedient to the movement of the Spirit.

All her suffering was for others, and as she was offered from the first instant of her existence, the Liturgy of blood that was to be consummated on Calvary began for her at her conception.

It is not within our power to follow all the development or trace all the upward movements of her love.

Think for a moment of the anguish of Joan of Arc at the pity of the realm of France, or the agony of Catherine of Siena at the wounds of the Church: and you will have some faint conception of the burning solicitude in the heart of the Virgin.

If you have ever seen a nun bending over the bed of a dying man left by his own to his misery, and uttering the words which give him back his childhood, you will have a figure of the maid of Nazareth, bending over a world in agony with all the tenderness of a charity which suffers immeasurably more from its compassion than the sufferer from his disease: for she knows what is the disease with which all are ill and who must be the Victim for all their wounds.

Despised and the most abject of men,
A man of sorrows and acquainted with infirmity;
And his look was as it were hidden and despised,
Whereupon we esteemed him not.
Surely he hath borne our infirmities
And carried our sorrows;
And we have thought of him as it were a leper,
And as one struck by God and afflicted.
But he was wounded for our iniquities,
He was bruised for our sins;
The chastisement of our peace was upon him
And by his bruises we are healed. (Is. liii. 3-5)

She could not read the words without being overwhelmed by distress, recognising in opprobrium the secret of His life, though she did not yet know that it would be as His mother that she would see the torment of the Man of Sorrows upon whom

Yahweh has caused to fall all our iniquity.

When she stood at the foot of the Cross, she saw all the instants of her life converging towards this unique moment in which she must take into herself the death agony of God.

The synoptic gospels tell us, with an objectivity equal to their reserve, the state of abandonment to which the soul of Jesus was delivered "When his hour was come." They make us see that His death was a torment inflicted by no human hand and that it gained His body only after crucifying His soul.

Comment would be as futile as sacrilegious. St. Paul has said the one word which could cast light upon those depths:

He was made sin for us.[1]

[1] Cf. II Cor. v. 21. What it says is: Him that knew no sin, for us he hath made sin, that we might be made the justice of God in Him.

There is the ineffable centre of the mystery. Jesus *felt* himself identified with Evil—whose horror He knew in the vision of God—felt himself as made to bear the responsibility for all man's denials of God, felt their appalling reality so laid upon Him that his very executioners may have seemed to have less guilt than He was bearing in the infinite anathema that was crushing Him down.[1]

All the beatific brightness shining at the summit of His spirit, all the holiness of His love, could but render more torturing this death-clutch of the darkness which held His soul so inexorably.

The evening before, His bodily senses had uttered all their distress in the sweat of blood, and now He breathes forth His soul in the cry which beat upon Mary's heart with the shattering force of a divine catastrophe:

My God, my God, why hast Thou forsaken Me? (Matt. xv. 34)

What part had she in His darkness?

It would be rash to make any affirmation what-

[1] Cf. Fr. Vincent McNabb, O. P., *From a Friar's Cell,* pp. 176, 191. This true theologian shows with admirable penetration the obscurity to which the *acquired* knowledge of Jesus might be subjected, and the suffering of which it might be the source. I have never read anything which shed so much light on an episode that one cannot think of save in trembling.

Gerard David

soever. Yet we may at least remind ourselves that Mary lived by faith and not in the face to face vision of God.

She believed, she did not see.

She had, we may be sure, received the most certain assurances of the mystery which had been accomplished within her. Yet its reality was for her not an object of knowledge but of faith.

May it have been by the fissure which lies between faith and sight that she was invaded by the darkness which submerged the soul of her Son? If so, she did not cease to adhere with unshakable certainty to the Word which had always been her guide.

Yet it seems that if such a trial were reserved for her, as is probable, it was not at this moment.

Her share had still, it would appear, an exclusively maternal character. As other women bring to the dying the luminous gift of supreme tenderness, she brought a mother's heart to the death agony of God. And she alone realised the immensity of the tragedy which centred all human history in the crucifixion of Love.

God died and He was her Son:
And she was His mother.

The one being who could be with Him, she stood

erect in her inviolable solitude, offering her innocence as witness of His, making all His opprobrium
wholly her own, stricken with all our denials, suffering the pain of all His wounds.

He looked upon her. He saw her sorrowing in
all His sorrows, pierced through with His distress,
bearing in all her being the wound of Love pitilessly
condemned. In a creation rebellious from its beginning, she at least was wholly His.

And He gave her to us: *Behold thy Mother.*

In this He really made her His mother in each of
us: *Mater pulchrae dilectionis:* Mother of Beautiful
Love; but in what an abyss of sorrow she received
the title.

For her we are ever the children of the *Stabat.*
She is bound to us with the same love which binds
her to Him. So she stands as long as the divine agony
endures.[1] She hastens to us to take Him down from
the Cross of whose torment our egoism is the daily,
hourly, renewal.

It is so that she sees all, in that terrible greatness
in which each one of us appears as responsible for
her Son, responsible for the blood that was shed,
responsible for the reign of love whose price He was.

It is so that she loves us in the eternal wisdom in

[1] "Jesus will be in agony till the end of the world, we must not
sleep the while." Pascal.

which man takes on his true face, in the light of that sacred Face whose ineffable mystery she presents to us: as the light of the candle in which the whole world lives anew.

> *Lumen Christi,*
> *Deo gratias!*
> *Light of Christ,*
> *Thanks be to God.*

V

The Monstrance of Jesus

As we look upon the spectacle of millions of men resolved to extirpate all religion, stretching out their hand over all frontiers with a sort of messianic fervour, we are driven to think of the man who was going down from Jerusalem to Damascus to bind up the disciples of Christ and destroy His name.

He was in good faith, he believed that the new sect was the incarnation of blasphemy and that he was bound in conscience to prevent it from spreading. The indomitable energy he felt boiling in his veins left him in no doubt upon the issue of his mission: he would put an end to an execrable superstition.

Yet before his journey was over, he had become its most flaming apostle.

He had suddenly understood. He had seen. All stood clear in the light of a Presence which took possession of him wholly, a Person who became his Life.

The first of many souls whom his word was to
enkindle, and more profoundly than they, he had
"put on" Christ, and His name was never to cease
to sound on his lips like a cry of love.

The lightning illumination of his meeting with
our Lord had revealed to him the solidarity or rather
the mysterious identity between Him whose love
had struck him down and the Community it had
been his dream to destroy:

"I am Jesus whom thou persecutest" (Acts ix. 5).
He had come to know as united and inseparable

Jesus in the Church
The Church in Jesus.

All his theology was to be the development of that
first truth which was for him the key to the Gospel:

Jesus and the Church are one:
The Church is Jesus.

If we had more care to efface self in Him, our
brethren might come to see in Him the truth they
seek, the justice they thirst for, and the love which
would transfigure their lives.

Could they resist the fascination He has for every
sincere soul, if the Church was always seen *in us*
with the face of Christ Jesus?

Yet this is the strict truth, and faith gives us an ever more living awareness of it:

We are in the Church only in the measure that we are in Jesus.

Like sacraments which in differing degrees symbolise Him or give Him to us, persons and rites, dogmas and laws all converge towards Him, to seal in Him all the powers of our being made subject to His love by an identification that grows ever closer—to the point where all our life is in Christ Jesus.

Thus Christianity comes to be seen by us increasingly as a Person, into whose intimacy it is the Church's mission to bring us.

So that we are sure, in the nature of the case, to find Jesus at the centre of all the doctrines that treat of the Virgin, His mother and ours.

What is externally visible sometimes leads into error even observers in good faith, anxious to come at the truth.

Love knows no measure in its language, it lives on hyperbole with a sort of instinct for totality which admits no reserve, just as there should be no reserve, nothing held back, in the gift man makes of himself to God.

What else—except this gift—is so good a witness

to our mystical vocation: as it were a fleeting antici-
pation, a rough but stimulating and intoxicating
sketch of that plenitude in which the whole being
attains its consummation in perfect altruism.

We race ahead, hurl ourselves towards the goal,
slake our thirst in the river of beatitude. What language can we speak save the language of adoration,
all dazzled with the infinite we feel before us?

And if the heart remains open and we love one
of God's creatures, then provided the loved being
does not fill the whole horizon, if he is but the translucid sign of a Presence beyond him so that our love
does not stop in him but reaches onward to that
Other, the essential order is not harmed but
strengthened.

The reality of the immediate object of our love
makes the reality of the Sovereign Good more vivid
to us, and both by its limits and its excellences leads
us on to It. Our words go beyond it, winging
towards that Light in which adoration finds its true
object.

We must never forget the dynamism inherent in
the proper use of creatures, if we are rightly to
evaluate the enthusiasm of the Christian love for the
Mother of Christ.

The Virgin does indeed truly represent something

supreme, but in the created order, and her transparence is that of a sacrament which cannot but bring us to God.

So that all the homage that rises up to her, like all the doctrines that express our belief about her, is strictly Christo-centric.

From this point of view there is no more moving object for our study than the dogma of the Immaculate Conception.

It is altogether astonishing to find coming from the pen of a Doctor who always had the name of Mary on his lips and in his heart, the letter St. Bernard wrote to the Canons of Lyons in protest against the Feast of the Conception recently introduced by them into the Cathedral liturgy.

"The glorious (Virgin)," he cries, "would choose to be without that honour by which one seems either to honour sin or to introduce a false sanctity. Assuredly she could find no pleasure against the custom of the Church—in a presumptuous novelty, mother of temerity, sister of superstition, daughter of light-mindedness.

"I had already been warned that this error was held by some, but I kept silence to spare the fervour that comes from a simple heart, full of love for the Virgin. But now, discovering the superstition among the learned, in a noble and famous church of which I am in a special sense the son, I know not if I can continue silent without doing you yourselves grave injury."

Earlier in the letter he had given the reason for his indignation:

"Though it has been given to some men—though very few—to be born in holiness, yet it has not been given to them to be conceived in holiness, in order that the prerogative of a holy conception should be reserved *to one alone*—to Him who was to sanctify all others and who, alone coming without sin, was to accomplish our purification from sin.

"Thus only the Lord Jesus has been conceived of the Holy Ghost, because only He was holy before His conception. Apart from Him, that is true of all the sons of Adam which one of them humbly and truthfully confessed of himself: 'In iniquity I was conceived, in sin my mother conceived me.' "[1]

St. Bernard happened to be wrong. But it would be impossible to find clearer evidence of the truth that love of Mary can never attribute anything to her that would derogate from the primacy of Jesus.

The great scholastics of the thirteenth century—Alexander of Hales, St. Albert the Great, St. Bona-

[1] Ep. clxxiv.

venture, St. Thomas Aquinas, were to adopt a position similar to St. Bernard's for the same motive.

All of course accepted what St. Augustine wrote in his book on Nature and Grace (Chapter xxxvi): "Of the Blessed Virgin Mary, for the honour of Christ, when we treat of sin I do not wish that she should be involved. For we know that a greater grace was accorded her wholly to conquer sin, by the very fact that she merited to conceive and bear Him of whom we certainly know that He had no sin."[1]

They were all in accord with St. Anselm: "It is fitting that the Virgin should be resplendent with a purity such that none could be conceived more perfect save only God's."[2]

They would all have accepted St. Thomas's own words: "More grace was granted to the Blessed Virgin that to any the saints. She was purer of all sin than all the saints. Upon the Blessed Virgin something was necessarily conferred beyond the general law. Her sanctification (from before her birth) was more perfect than that of others. We must hold that all that could be accorded to her was in fact accorded. It is altogether probable that she who bore the only Son of the Father, full of grace

[1] Quoted Del Prado, *Divus Thomas et Bulla dogmatica Ineffabilis Deus*, p. 208.
[2] *De conceptu Virginali*, cap XVIII.

and truth, in preference to all others received greater privileges and graces."[1]

And all would have applauded the Angelic Doctor's exegesis of Psalm xviii. 6 ("He hath set my tabernacle in the sun")[2]: "This means that Christ caused His body to rest in the sun, that is in the Blessed Virgin who had no darkening of sin, according to the word of the Canticle: 'Thou art all beautiful, my beloved, there is no spot in thee.'"

What they would not allow was that she had in no way contracted the necessity of a personal redemption. For, following the remark of St. Bonaventure, "it concerns the eminent dignity of Christ that He should be the Redeemer and Saviour of all, that He opened to all the gate (of life) and that He alone died for all. We must certainly not withdraw the Blessed Virgin Mary from the general application (of this law) lest by augmenting the glory of the mother we diminish the glory of the Son and thereby provoke the Mother, whose wish it is that her Son should be exalted above herself, the Creator above the creature."[3]

[1] III *Sent.*, dist. 3, q.1, a.1 and *S. T.* III[a], q.27, a.1.

[2] See Del Prado, *op. cit.*, p. 110.

[3] III *Sent.*, dist. 3, p.1, a.1, q.2; quoted by Del Prado, *op. cit.*, 174-6.

Père Del Prado, in relating this great theological epopee, shows admirably that the formal object of the resistance of the great Doctors was always and solely to safeguard the *universal* redemptive primacy

As they held, with the whole of tradition, that the Virgin had never been guilty of any actual fault, it remained that she must in some manner have incurred original sin.

As she could not be personally redeemed before existing and thus entering into solidarity with Adam, it was concluded that she must have been sanctified after her soul was created and united to her body.

Yet even so early St. Bonaventure suggested that this "after" might imply posteriority of nature only, and need not exclude simultaneity in time.

Scotus brought the question a stage forward by introducing the idea of a debt—or, if you prefer, an exigence, a necessity from which its effect must issue unless some intervention from above prevented.

Cajetan clarified this notion with incisive rigour by recalling (what St. Thomas had taught) that the necessity of *dying,* affirmed *de jure,* of all the children of Adam, does not mean that *de facto* a special

---

of Jesus, by affirming the *personal* redemption of Mary, because the question of the Immaculate Conception as it was stated in their day left this point obscure. We can see that this was so if we weigh attentively the words of St. Bernard in the fragment of his letter we have quoted. It should therefore not be said that they were opponents of the dogma as it has now been defined but rather that they were safeguarding its Christocentrism.

disposition of Providence might not exempt some particular individual from death. "If anyone did not personally incur original sin, either in fact, or in the necessity of having it, he would have no need of redemption. It suffices to render redemption necessary that all should be under the debt of original sin."[1]

Therefore to bring the Virgin within the redemptive action of Christ, it was sufficient to affirm that in the instant she came into personal existence, Mary bore in her (having regard to the totally human conditions of her generation) that exigence inherent in fallen nature and running counter to the divine life which would have separated her from God, if *at the same instant* a superabundance of grace had not prevented that effect.

Which is equivalent to saying that in the first moment of her existence she was under the necessity of incurring original sin, of being deprived of the divine ordination of grace, by virtue of the mysterious solidarity of which carnal propagation is the vehicle; yet at the same time she was withdrawn from this necessity by redemptive grace, in virtue of the infinitely higher and more efficacious solidarity which ordered her to Jesus as His mother. Upon

[1] Del Prado, *op. cit.*, 95, 96.

this statement of the truth, the Christian mind gradually settled. It had given itself time to ripen.

Piety had already found what it needed in the celebration of the feast of the Immaculate Conception, adopted in the Roman church as early as the thirteenth century, and vigorously defended by Pope Sixtus IV in the Constitutions of the years 1476 and 1483.[1]

The Council of Trent, mentioning these decisions, made them its own in 1546 by formally excepting the blessed and immaculate Virgin Mary from the decree on original sin.[2]

Yet on 4 July 1622 Gregory XV could declare: "The Holy Spirit, implored by the most urgent prayers, has not manifested to His Church the secret of such a mystery. And it is only under His guidance that we must read the scroll of eternity in the Chair of Christian Wisdom."[3]

On December 8, 1661, Alexander VII registered the progress of the belief "which almost all Catholics hold."[4]

On December 8, 1854, Pius IX's definition made it a dogma affirming that "prevented by the merits

[1] Denzinger, 12th ed., 734, 735.
[2] ibid., 792.
[3] Quoted Del Prado, op. cit., 102.
[4] Denzinger, 1100.

of Christ the Redeemer, Mary had not been subjected to original sin but entirely preserved from
its stain and because of this *redeemed in a more
sublime manner*." A Wisdom higher than that of the
Doctors had given a reply eminently satisfactory to
their wisdom, in that it underlined what they had
always kept in the forefront: the universally redemptive primacy of Christ Our Saviour.

The phrase of the Bull *Ineffabilis Deus*—"redeemed in a more sublime manner"—so to speak
canonised the Christocentrism which they had always
seen to be the essential point of the teaching upon
our Lady. Mary, wholly ordered to Jesus from the
first instant of her existence, identified with His Passion in the being of grace which made her the new
Eve, was thus wholly of the blood of Jesus, His
daughter according to the Spirit, before He was of
her blood according to the flesh in that ineffable
motherhood which was to be the eternal giving back
in love of all that she had received from Him.

Jesus triumphant in Mary: Mary made totally
His, conceived for Him and already prepared for
Him in the first instant of her existence: that fundamentally is what faith has come to see, giving to the
angelic salutation the plenitude of possible meaning:

Hail, full of grace, the Lord is with thee.

As in the Blessed Trinity, the Father *is* His Paternity, as a living relation to His Son, so likewise the Blessed Virgin draws, so to speak, all her personality from the ineffable relation which consecrates her wholly to that same Son, whom she bore in her flesh as the fruit of the Spirit.

> Mary is wholly
> Mary is solely
> Mary is from the beginning
> The Mother of Jesus.

As in the Virgin's beginning all is ruled by her interior life with a view to her divine maternity, so also it is with her death.

Having regard to the purely spiritual economy of her being, she did not have to die; if it is true, as Paul teaches so profoundly, that death is the wages of sin.[1]

The true God, indeed, is the God of the *living*.[2] It is not He who invented death. Death results from that *absence* which man has opposed to His *Presence* since that early day when the father of the human race chose to turn away from the Source to build his life wholly upon himself.

He had thus cast the human race of which he

[1] Rom. v. 12.
[2] Matt. xxii, 32.

was the head and representative into the cosmic adventure, since by reason of its position upon the frontier of matter and spirit it could give the preference to either.[1]

Thus the living sources in man were affected: a sort of practical primacy was conferred upon the body, which was to subject the soul to its rhythm. In the most fortunate cases, life would move inward from without, painfully re-establishing the domination over its centrifugal tendencies by an interiority painfully maintained. Henceforth the flesh, stiffened in its resistance to spirit, would accept spirit's yoke with difficulty: and its resistance would set resounding in the whole of man's being that "answer of death" of which the Apostle speaks.[2]

The body is too exterior to the soul ever to be entirely dominated by the soul and rendered completely obedient to its control. The supreme absence has its repercussion in the body until its precariously held autonomy[3] vanishes in death: where it must await the mystery of the resurrection.

[1] Though obviously he has the moral obligation, inscribed in his very essence, of giving the preference to the spirit by subordinating the body to it: which is the supreme way of loving the body, since it makes it participate in a higher life.

[2] II Cor. i. 9.

[3] This "autonomy" of the body is one of the effects of the great refusal at the beginning of man's history: it deprived man's faculties of their supreme equilibrium in their divine centre, by a sort of dispersion which leaves in each a tendency to make itself the centre to the detriment of all the others.

But in Mary there could be no question of absence from God: whether in her soul which was wholly given to Him, or in her body which was the cradle of the Word made flesh. Her life was wholly sealed within the eternal order of Love.

Thus death could not result in her from any inner disorder of her being. Death could come to her only from the spirit, in an act of supreme conformity to Christ the Redeemer. She died, we can be certain, in prayer, listening to the Voice which commanded every fibre of her being, answering the call which found her always prepared:

Come from Libanus, my spouse,
Come from Libanus, come. (Cant. iv. 8)

She died of love. She entered into the light which she had borne in her womb:

She *saw* that she was the Mother of God.[1]

Yet her body, which in every fibre had never ceased to be present to the Life which was born of her, contained in itself an exigency for resurrection. Like her soul, it was wholly ordered to Jesus.

It was rejoined to her soul that the kingdom of

[1] Scheeben *Dogm.* III, 570-588.

Christ should be accomplished in the one as in the other.

We can make no image of that resurrection, or of the wholly supernatural manner in which a "spiritual body" must live. The functioning of corporal matter is known to us under the condition of exteriority which makes it a limit to spirit; we do not know what it can be under the condition of interiority which makes it the expression of spirit[1]—when, denuded of its illusion of autonomy, it too has entered into the divine poverty.

If one cannot be without acting, what can be the activity of Mary, so profoundly ordered to Jesus, if not to express Him as the Word of her heart, and to draw all to Him by bringing Him to birth in all those who are to live by Him?

That Mary should give us Jesus and should obtain for us all that makes Him live in us, that is what we mean by calling her Mediatrix of All Graces: which means nothing but this—that she is always, in her relations with Him and her relations with us, the Mother of Jesus. Just as her being has Christ for its centre, so has her action. Her influence is wherever the Saviour is to come to dwell, wherever there shines any reflection of His life. That is to say

[1] Cf. Maurice Blondel, *La Pensée*, II, 479.

she is universal—according to her own mode, which is to efface herself in Jesus. So that her unique aim is to produce in us a union ever more immediate and personal with Jesus.

We know from experience that as genius is purer and virtue more perfect, they tend the more to quicken our true personality by communicating to us something of their own intimacy with the Light.

The infinite transparence of the Virgin can have no other effect than to develop such a transparence in us, that the brightness of the Word may flood in upon us wholly.

She is not our last end, but she is the sacrament by which our last end sets energizing in us its luminous magnetism. She renders our being ever more present to God, ever more interior to the life of Jesus, as we are more filially receptive to her maternal influence.

But she does not intervene in that supreme communion in which the soul, face to face with its Lord —in the night of this life or the morning of the beatific vision—hears the unique word which stirs in it the unique response by which is consummated the ineffable union that God contracted with it in the mysterious espousals of baptism.

She is not the Source but the "aqueduct"[1] through

---

[1] St. Bernard, *Sermo de aquaeductu in Nativ. B. V. Mariae.*

which the Source flows to us; she is not Wisdom but the Seat of Wisdom; she is not Life but the enclosed garden in which the river of Life springs up.

In her, as in the Church, it is always Jesus we meet:[1]

I, Jesus, have sent my angel. . . .
I am the root and stock of David,
The bright and morning star.
And the spirit and the bride say: Come.
And he that heareth, let him say: Come.
And he that thirsteth, let him come
And he that will, let him take the water of life
*   freely.* (Apoc. xxii. 16, 17)

Just as the great cathedrals, under the name of Our Lady, are tabernacles of the Host, so Mary gleams in the Church as His Monstrance.

---

[1] Because He comes to meet us in her, as He went in her to meet Elizabeth and John in the mystery of the Visitation.

VI

God Is Love

ALMOST all men wear a mask which they have put on instinctively to defend the secret of their soul.[1] It becomes so habitual to them that they forget to take it off even when they are alone, and they end by no longer knowing the true face that is their own. Their soul is like a sealed book to itself. They live under constraint and seek liberation in excesses which are a new outrage to their nature.

Many who cannot thus escape really, give rein to their imagination. For many existence is a precarious, ceaselessly menaced, equilibrium of obligations, true or feigned, whose performance constitutes their social being.

The idea men have of them is a prison walling them in, the circles in which they live require that they shall conform: conventions of family, school, newspaper, party; professional, national, religious slogans: there is no way of escaping the tyranny of what is or is not done.

[1] Cf. Charles Morgan, *The Fountain*. " 'I am alone,' he repeated, as if by repetition of the word he could ensure the privacy of his soul."

Le Maître de Moulins

Only that society closes its eye to the flesh's adventures—provided the rules of the game are observed—and divinises every muscular exploit to give a semblance of nourishment to the appetite for glory that devours us, life would be given utterly to despair.

There are artists who seek to exorcise this despair by urging us to *suck all the sweetness* of the passing instant. No remedy could be more remote from reality. It assumes the agreement of the greater number: unless you are prepared to taylorise pleasure and make lust a department of state.

There is more hope in the plain fact that humanity is beginning to weary of this ceaseless drawing upon its nerves and muscles.

Those who still resort to this kind of thrill are rather in search of an anodyne than in expectation of joy. They want to kill time, above all to forget, as the sole way of escape from the vertigo of the grief within them. And when the poor thrill is past, their bodies are heavier and there is only bitterness in their faces and a piercing distress in the depths of their eyes.

What then prevents them from turning away from this death and finding the way of life?

They have experienced so often the nothingness of pleasures which blunt desire and leave hunger unappeased. They do not need the lights we have in order to realise how short is this animal satisfaction.

But their sense of liberty is atrophied: they no longer know that they can do as they will with themselves, that they possess the divine faculty of self-giving.

Almost always duty has been presented to them as a constraint, under the mortifying label of repression.

They were called upon for acts conformable to an abstract rule, and there was no effort to establish in them the order of love, starting from a principle within their own souls.

Yet surely it must be clear that the root of all impurity is the spirit of *possession* in the disordered love of self, as the spirit of *poverty* is the source of all rightness in the God-centred life of Charity.

The most perfect conformity—like that of the Pharisees denounced by Jesus—may be profoundly immoral.

Without love, works are nothing.[1]

Which does not mean that works are not necessary in the service of love; but that love is the alpha and omega of the whole moral life.

[1] Cf. "Chastity without charity shall be chained in hell"—*The Vision of Piers Plowman*.

One may be obliged, of course, to impose an external discipline, to defend a social order, against the anarchy which would render life in common impossible; but to limit the mind to that discipline and order would be a betrayal of the Spirit.

No act except loving God can fill full that capacity for the infinite which orders our will to the sovereign Good.

It is therefore an outrage against our liberty to tie it down within the rules of what is done and what is not done: unless all our action is identified with love as its expression.

God's commandments have no other object than to introduce into the diversity of action the spirit of poverty which gives to every use of the creature the transparence of a giving. They seek to keep us from being immersed in external activity, from being imprisoned in the partial, from desiring less than the infinite. That is why Jesus can sum them all up in the one commandment:

Thou shalt love.

That they so often stir us to revolt is due to the wholly material understanding we have of them. In breaking them, our fundamental aim is not so much the sin we do as the affirmation of our own autonomy.

But what good can the will discover in activity

in which its true good is not, in which its spiritual dignity[1] and immeasurable amplitude are betrayed?

It can be conquered only with its own consent, under the attraction of a love which separates it from self.

It is only love in truth which can without violence incline toward another the free disposition of self, causing it to attach itself to the excellence of the loved being as the most perfect expression of its own interiority, the true achievement of its autonomy.

Therefore it is only in the infinite respect shown to his mystery that man can recognise at once the greatness of his soul and who it is that alone can fill it full: God, whom obscurely it has felt everywhere without being able to name Him. In the act of faith you make in all that a man can become beyond what he may actually be; in the homage you

---

[1] "Only love can make the soul pleasing to God" (str. 28) . . . "God is pleased with nothing but love . . . All our works, and all our labours, how grand soever they may be, are nothing in the sight of God, for we can give him nothing, neither can we by them fulfil His desire, which is the growth of our soul . . . As there is no way in which the soul can grow but in becoming in a manner equal to Him, for this reason only is He pleased with our love. It is the property of love to place him who loves on an equality with the object of his love. Hence the soul, because of its perfect love is called the bride of the Son of God, which signifies equality with Him. In this equality and friendship, all things are common." (*The Mystical Doctrine of St. John of the Cross*, Sheed & Ward, p. 208.) "I do not wish to violate the laws of your liberty. But once you so desire, I transform you into Me and make you one with Me." (St. Catherine of Siena, *Dialogues*.)

pay to all that the grace of God can accomplish in him; in your willingness to accept what he is and the unique character of the function he is called to fulfil; in your refraining from judgment and from any interference with his conscience beyond what he himself invites; in the reserve, in short, in the silent adhesion to all that passes speech, the kneeling of your soul before his—in all this man feels infinite horizons opening before him and begins to breathe the air of his true country. He can be himself, he drops his mask, he shows you the true face of his nativity.

This is precisely what Jesus did when they brought to him the woman taken in adultery. He lowered his eyes not to look upon her shame, He allowed her to rediscover her own self in the silent love with which he enveloped her, He delivered her from the judgment of her accusers, scattering them with the voice of their own conscience. And when at last He looked at her, it was to utter words of divine respect:

"Hath no man condemned thee?"
"No man, Lord."
"Neither will I condemn thee. Go, and now sin no more."[1]

[1] John viii. 1-11.

Man can only be born from the womb of a mother. It is in tenderness that he enters into life. And it is in love, too, that he is born again:

"How can a man be born when he is old?" asks Nicodemus. "Can he enter a second time into his mother's womb?"[1]

In every event, his soul has need of a cradle. Everywhere he seeks the maternal heart in which his distress can find rest; and when he has found it, he begins to know what God is.

If we ask ourselves the question: What, of all our certitudes, at all the moments of our life, subsist unshakably not merely as an abstract conviction but as a living light and dynamic impulse?—there is surely only one possible reply: Our faith in the absolute value of goodness. We cannot open our being save to its contact, we meet other things only in its radiance.

The terrible fatality of the cosmic laws whose plaything man seems to be, the huge machine of misery in which he is caught and ground, all the horrible burden of lusting and coveting under which he is so shamefully crushed with the lightless connivance of a damaged will and the gnawing appetite of the senses—all this litter that cumbers life is exorcised in that instant when a flash of goodness

[1] John iii. 4.

makes us see the moral sense of the universe showing in a human face.

Thus there is in us a Value which nothing can attaint, which survives all that can happen to us, which is sufficient to itself: a Reality without which nothing has value, by which all darkness is made light, in which nothing is impossible to us; a Presence which makes us interior one to another, which transcends us yet liberates what is most personal in us, which subsists in itself yet cannot express itself in us without our consent; a living Goodness, which shows us goodness as the essence of our duty and our last end, by making us feel in the flowering of being it causes that all creation has its source in the goodness for which it yearns in its unawareness that it has been anticipated by eternal love:

> *In caritate perpetua dilexi te.*
> *With an everlasting love have I loved thee.*[1]

In truth, so long as a man can make his own the two lines of Verlaine's *Wisdom*:

> Go, nothing is better for the soul
> than to make another soul less sad—

[1] Jer. xxxi. 3.

he remains in contact with the essential Truth and
can hear with expectation the promises of Scripture:

Can a woman forget her infant,
So as not to have pity on the son of her womb?
And if she should forget,
Yet will I not forget thee. . . .[1]
Shall not I that make others to bring forth children,
Myself bring forth, saith the Lord.
Shall I, that give generation to others,
Be barren, saith the Lord thy God?
Rejoice with Jerusalem,
And be glad with her all you that love her:
Rejoice with joy for her, all you that mourn for her!
That you may suck and be filled
With the breasts of her consolations:
That you may milk out and flow with delights
From the abundance of her glory.
For thus saith the Lord:
Behold I will bring upon her as it were a river of
   peace,
And as an overflowing torrent, the glory of the
   gentiles.
You shall be carried at the breasts,
And upon the knees they shall caress you.

[1] Isaias XLIX. 15.

As one whom the mother caresseth,
So will I comfort you.[1]

This God with a mother's face—who would not tremble with joy to hear Him called by that name which is the loveliest synonym of all Goodness?

Given that he has created all by love and for love, to make us live his own Life—provided only that we give our consent—then obviously the thing He must ask of us as the one thing necessary is the total abandonment which puts us as new-born infants into His hands, that He may express in us, as in the transparence of His Word, the infinite riches of His love:

> *Quasi modo geniti infantes . . .*
> *As new born-babes*
> *desire the milk of the Word without guile.*
>   I Pet. ii. 2.

Nor is there any way in which He may bring us to this attitude of filial abandonment to Himself more effectively than by binding us to His heart by the heart of the Virgin, who is the great sacrament of the divine tenderness.

[1] Isaias LXVI. 9-13.

If every creature is *by what he is* the reflection of the divine being, how could Mary, who is wholly mother, reveal Him to us otherwise than as maternal; infinitely more so than she is herself, since He is the source of her tenderness and of the tenderness of all mothers.

What is the cause then of our sorrow and of the appalling devastation of evil which makes history one long agony?

Man's refusal, which has bound God's hand to the wood of torment where God must bear our blows, until we come for refuge into that Heart from which by the sword's piercing a river of life was made to flow.

We do not know how history is unrolled beyond the veil, in the unthinkable design hymned by the Father through His sole-begotten Word in the fire of the Spirit.

But we know enough of the actions of the Word made flesh to identify God eternally with "that Heart which so loved men."

But the Gospel of Mary, or rather the Gospel that Mary is, does not contain only the revelation of the Maternity of God, is not only our guarantee that we are at every instant the fruit of God's tenderness, and that in us also—according to the degree in which

we open our soul—is realised the word which set
the first Christmas sky ablaze with the brightness of
the true Light:[1]

> *The Lord said to me: Thou art my Son*
> *This day have I begotten thee.*[2]

In giving birth to God, the Virgin revealed in her
own maternity the utterly ineffable Maternity of
God.

We must do likewise,[3] since God has loved us
enough to want to receive from us a further humanity.

There are no words to utter this, but the heart
can hear it as it contemplates in Jesus and Mary the
most exquisite human experience.

A little girl had come out with her mother to see
the sun set. Evening gradually spread its silence over
the vineyards. The lake was motionless as a gaze of

---

[1] Collect for Christmas, midnight.

[2] Introit for Christmas, midnight.

[3] "The Saviour," says the Venerable Bede, "approves in felicitous
words the exclamation of the woman [who had said Blessed is the
womb that bore thee] by affirming not only that she was blessed who
had merited to bear the Word of God corporeally, but that they also
were blessed who strove to conceive the same word spiritually in the
understanding of faith, and to give Him birth and nourish Him, by
the practice of good, in their own heart and the heart of their neigh-
bour" (*Comm. Fest. beatae Mariae Virginis*, 3rd Nocturn).

contemplation in the fiery ring of the mountains. The whole earth seemed to chant the hymn of life.

The two walked on through all this glory without a word. Suddenly, in the intoxication of so much beauty, and finding no word to render thanks for so much joy, the child embraced her mother saying: "You are born of my heart."

It is an analogous restitution, only infinitely more real, that the divine love proposes to us: He has willed to be born in us *of* us, that His life in us should be the fruit of our love and the accomplishment of our fecundity:

"For whosoever shall do the will of my Father, that is in heaven, he is my brother and my sister and my mother."[1]

Thus there is in some sort a solidarity between His destiny in the universe and ours, and His poverty finds its consummation in His waiting upon us.

> *I stand at the gate and knock*
> *If any man shall hear my voice,*
> *And open to me the door,*
> *I will come in to him.*[2]

In the measure in which we hear this appeal, we shall know the true face of man.

[1] Matt. XII. 50.   [2] Apoc. III. 20.

Creation cannot come to achievement in any man unless he consents. From this point of view, which is ultimate, every man has an infinite value, and every beat of every man's heart is indispensable to the accomplishment of the Kingdom of God.

Our most material relations with our fellows put us in some way in contact with souls. We open the door or close it, we let God pass through or bar Him out.

Men would not kill men so lightly if they knew with what they had to do. They would see that *a person* is of itself worth more than all the material wealth of the world, *by reason of Christ who is committed to him.*

No problem can be solved apart from this truth, for it is only at this level that man finds himself.

Contemplation has God for its centre, but so has all life. In every being our love must prepare a cradle for the Word who does not wish to cease to be born in the world:

> *Unto us a Child is born*
> *Unto us a Son is given.*[1]

How powerfully must Vincent de Paul have felt this truth as he gathered up for God those whom

[1] Introit for Christmas Third Mass during Day.

men had cast out, or Francis of Assisi when he sent
Brother Angelo to beg pardon of the brigands whom
he had sent off with insufficient respect!

It is in truth a very high manner of uniting our-
self to God when, after having fed our soul upon
the sacred Liturgy, we make our prayer upon our
brethren,[1] considering the majesty of Christ who
covers them with honour. I know no prayer more
simple and urgent and practical, nor one that cor-
responds more closely with the Testament of the
Lord:

*A new commandment I give unto you: that you
love one another, as I have loved you.* (John xiii. 34)

It was, we may assume, in order to give this com-
mand its perfect fulfilment that Mary remained with
the new-born church after the Saviour's ascension,
aiding each to realise in regard to each what Saul

---

[1] The same may be said of the prayer that each can make upon himself, in so far as he is himself in his own hand as placed there by
Christ. (Cf. Bremond, *Histoire du sentiment religieux* II, 278, 279.)

Aristotle taught long ago that the will can exercise over the faculties
which depend upon it a domination not despotic but politic merely:
man must not handle himself like a package of goods, he must treat
himself with patience, prudence and reverence, in the humility of a
charity whose care is to offer all his powers to God. He must not put
himself to a tension too great, and thus accumulate futile repressions.
Simply he must give all that he has in himself to dispose of, remaining open to all that can make him more capable of giving himself.

was to learn of all the members in the unity of the Head: "I am Jesus whom thou persecutest."

She has not ceased since to pour out upon the faithful that same maternal solicitude, keeping alive in their hearts, in the illumination of the gift of wisdom, that morning light of knowledge by which all is known in the Word, who is the Son of the Father and the Son of Mary, and who must be born of us too in the measure in which we efface our selves in Him:

like the Poor Woman
who bears in her heart
the eternal Wisdom from which Love proceeds.[1]

[1] "And where there is no love, put love and you will draw forth love." Baruzi, *Saint Jean de la Croix*, 2nd ed., p. 218.

EPILOGUE

WISDOM AND POVERTY

ON THE night when St. Francis had the vision of the Seraph which marked his flesh with the mysterious seal of the martyrdom of love which identified him with the Saviour, Mount Alverno blazed so bright that all the hills and valleys round shone with its light.

Seeing the mountain ablaze, shepherds guarding their flocks were terrified; and in the inns of that region muleteers bound for the Romagna woke with a start thinking that day had come, and saddled their beasts and started on their way.

But as they journeyed on they saw that light disappear, and the material sun rise which had been anticipated by the miraculous dawn of a flaming ecstasy.

Thus a divine light attested the gospel of fire written in the stigmata of the crucified follower of his Lord.

When Francis came down from the mountain, he could hardly bear to put his torn feet to the ground. His brethren observed that he kept his hands hidden in his sleeves, and on his tunic was a great stain of blood at the level of his heart.

And Alverno seemed to them like another Sinai. It is in this light that it will always be seen by those who have begun to find some savour in the folly of the Cross.

That a God should die the death of love after having suffered judgment and condemnation by the creature, is in last resort the only unanswerable answer to the appalling reality of evil.

Why does God allow the triumph of our weakness, cowardice, denial with its resulting abysses of sorrow? Why does He not intervene?

When a man comes to see in the centre of history the hill of Calvary and to realise the dreadful reality of the agony beyond words suffered upon it, he feels the wounds of man no less vividly than before, but he does at last begin to understand with what supreme compassion he should look upon the wounds of God. And it is then that he turns, with all the power of his heart, to the little poor man who came down from Mount Alverno bearing the marks of the Great Poor Man, "not figured upon tables of stone or wood by the hand of the artist, but inscribed upon his bodily members by the finger of the living God."

There are philosophers[1] who have a totally exterior, abstract and mechanical idea of being, and who in their simplicity imagine that the arguments by which they arrive at the existence of God put them in a privileged position as compared with the rank and file of believers. And these philosophers have given us a very different idea of God.

Relying principally on physical considerations and denuding their thought of all spiritual vitality, they have conceived God's elevation as a kind of remoteness, seeing Him as external to the universe whose sole reason He is, and obviously thinking that His perfection shone all the more brightly therefor; whereas the truth is the reverse—that He is closer, more interior to every being precisely because He is the infinite plenitude of life, totally sufficing to itself, since "in Him we live and move and have our being."

How should He be remote from us, He who is the life-giving air that our being breathes?

---

[1] Among whom one must be on one's guard against figuring once one comes forth from recollection to engage in argumentation.

Therefore we must not say that He is exterior, when it is we who have become exterior to Him.

If it is true that He is absolutely distinct from us, this does not mean by a separation in space—for space has no hold upon Him—but by our imperfection in which He has no part.

And in truth His elevation, which the philosophers call His trancendence, results from the infinite purity and simplicity of His being, from His supreme immateriality—that is, in one word, His *perfect interiority*. He is pure interiority, a pure within, whereas every creature in its degree is external to itself as well as internal.

Examples will aid us to see this aspect of the problem, whose spiritual resonances will soon appear.

"We are not content," says Pascal,[1] "with the life we have in us and in our own being, we want to live in the minds of others with an imaginary life, and we put all our effort into appearance. We work unceasingly to preserve and beautify our imaginary being, the picture others have of us, and we neglect our real being."

This means simply that vanity is the betrayal of

[1] *Pensées,* ed. Brunschvig, no. 147.

our appetite for glory, as impurity of our appetite for life and pride of our appetite for greatness.

Thus our vices, causing our instincts to deviate from their goal, mutilate our being and render it exterior to itself.

We may observe similar analogies in the domain of Knowledge. We often meet even in cultivated minds a superficial spiritualizing just sufficient to confer the prestige of the absolute upon ambition and falsehood, upon injustice and sensuality, upon all that is furthest from spiritual values and most exterior to truth; for truth is the inner being of things coming to ripeness in the inner being of the mind, by the application of our mind to the *thought* that is latent in everything like a veiled ray of the divine light.

Error like evil is an absence of reality. If we are capable of both, it is because we are in a certain manner *exterior* to being, because our inner structure contains a fissure whereby we can issue towards nothingness. If we were Being, if we could say "I am who am," we should be God and so Truth itself. But since we are not God and Truth itself, and yet we exist, we must be distinct from God in that we remain exterior to the fullness of being which is

His, distinct from Him as a being from Being, re-
flecting His light on the opaque surface of a being
mingled with nothingness, as a mirror reflects the
sun only by intercepting its rays.

To each one of us can be applied the word which
revealed to St. Catherine of Siena what it is that
distinguishes creature from Creator: "You are that
which is not."

If you stop short at yourself, seeking to know
who you are and your true name, you will be
stupefied at your impotence to seize yourself, to
identify yourself perfectly in that centre of your
being that is always wrapped about with darkness.
And this will be an evidence to you of the mysterious fissure within your being which as it were
puts you outside yourself.

This paradoxical situation is in any event inevit-
able. The creature can exist really only by being
made mysteriously exterior to God by that element
of limitation which keeps its essence to a determined
and hence finite capacity of being.

Call this element of limitation shadow, potentiality, matter, existent non-being, what you please.
The point to grasp is that it is in us—and propor-
tionally in every creature—the principle of all that
disperses and diffuses us in becoming, the principle

also of all error, all failing, all materiality—in short of all that I have called exteriority.

But it must not be thought that our nature, our essence, our aptitude for being, is wholly given over to that dispersion by which it moves outward from its source.

The word revealed to St. Catherine—"You are that which is not"—must be read in the light of another word divinely attested—"Let us make man in our image and likeness."

In this aspect we are akin to our Creator, drawn as with a magnet to our true end by His being, in which there is no limitation of essence, nor dispersion in time, nor diffusion in space, nor any shadow of potentiality, nor any exteriority of matter, but the pure interiority of one unique Act, in the ineffable recollection of a duration without succession.

Against the current that would bear us outward to diffusion arises a current that bears us inward to recollection. It is this current that we call the interior *life*.

There is no need to consider here what that life might be if it had remained purely natural. For God has chosen for us a supernatural order.[1] We

[1] This must never be forgotten in the living contact with souls: the divine revelation is in some manner prefigured in them by grace which works upon them in secret. The prime necessity is to ensure the

have seen that our existence cannot be conceived save as exterior to His being. But He has been so far from wishing to confine us within this exteriority, that though we are *by nature*, by the primordial exigency of our being, creatures, He has chosen *by grace* to make us gods.[1]

He has been so little jealous of the privileges of His essence that He has set working in our souls, by the divine ferment of sanctifying grace, all the organism of the virtues and gifts to implant within us the supreme interiority of His nature and His life: *Aedificans Jerusalem Dominus dispersiones Israelis congregabit—The Lord buildeth up Jerusalem; he will gather together the dispersed of Israel*. (Ps. cxlvi. 2)

But God alone will not effect this interiorisation of all our powers which gathers them from their dispersion to render them capable of the exercise in us of His life. In order that this life should be fully our life too, it must be ratified by our consent and develop with our collaboration:

---

coincidence of what we must teach them of sacred doctrine with the ray of interior light which will make it divinely legible for them.

[1] The opposition of nature and grace might be stated summarily in this: by nature we are creatures, by grace we become God—on the understanding, of course, that the elevation expressed by the second term does not cancel the dependence expressed by the first. Otherwise the creature would disappear, and with it all the reality of the *gift* of God.

For I have espoused you to one husband, that I may present you as a chaste virgin to Christ. (II Cor. xi. 2)

He has chosen to enter into a marriage of love with us in which, by an ineffable equality, our yes is as necessary as His. Thereby in a certain manner He makes us arbiters of our own destiny and submits Himself in some sort to our judgment:

And this is the judgment, because the light is come into the world, and men loved darkness rather than the light. (John iii. 19)

This is what we find so magnificently illustrated in the great cathedrals where the Last Judgment is shown as the justification of eternal love in the showing of the wounds in Christ's hands surrounded by the instruments of the Passion.

What is there that I ought to do more for thee, O my people, that I have not done. (Cf. Is. v. 4)

It is impossible to meditate upon this scene without coming to realise that justice is but the constancy of love as might is its radiance.

But we must go deeper and contemplate the very source of this love in the heart of the Most Holy Trinity.

It is here, perhaps, that the distance is greatest between the frigid speculations of an academic logic and the burning light of revelation.

Philosophers so often see God as no more than an abstract principle from which one has but to deduce the consequences mechanically, that they overlook the spiritual analogies which they could find in their own inner life—its initiative of liberty, its living balance and its ever-newness, its thirst for perfection made only keener by the experience of evil, its moral exigencies and the wealth of love that is in it.

Not that we must transfer all that to God and attribute it to Him just as it stands. But at least we can draw, from the consciousness of our own complexity, some sense of mystery; and can learn not to apply to the Ineffable a wholly mechanical dialectic which if applied to our own spiritual life would be seen as an intolerable profanation. Nothing is more wounding to a believing soul than the way in which too often the holiness of God is spoken of by constructors of systems in total disregard of mystical experience.

One sometimes wonders what relation there can be between this sort of metaphysical secretion, which certain of them give us as a fatal necessity written in the perfectly unbroken sphere of an eternal egocentrism, and on the other hand the dignity, fervour, purity, nobility, disinterestedness and unbought magnanimity of human holiness as manifested in those whom the Christian people venerate as saints.

It is true that reason could not of itself arrive at the truth that the disinterestedness, the fundamental altruism, the self-giving which characterise moral perfection among men, are in God, in the form of a subsistent relation, the determining reason of His *personal* life.

God knows Himself, God loves Himself, say the philosophers. But His "self" is a triple focus of eternal altruism, wherein the divine life is appropriated only by the communication made of it in the infinite *élan*—identical with the life itself[1]—by which each of the three persons gives to the two others all It has and all It is.

Thus it is that Being in its source is personified under the form of gift and that the supreme autonomy is constituted by an infinite altruism. This is what the first Epistle of St. John makes plain in revealing to us the secret of the Being who in *Exodus* named Himself as "I am who am":

And we have known, and have believed the charity which God hath to us [for] God is love. (I John iv. 16)

We can now see in how magnificent a sense it may be said that the divine life suffices perfectly to itself.

---

[1] As I was seeking some way to express the pure *élan* that each divine person is in the subsistant ordination of its self to the two others, trying to make up by clumsy phrases for the winged image that would not come, a poet offered me this: "as if a bird were only flight."

It does so not in the clutching enjoyment of an ego-centric plenitude of being, but in the eternal ecstasy of an outpouring wherein each self is distinguished from each other self, only by each giving itself totally to each, by an ineffable outpouring of itself which makes of each person a living altruism.

Thus are manifested in the pure interiority of the divine being the moral conditions of perfect holiness, in the ceaseless springing of a charity which finds in God himself the *élan* toward others which consecrates it and the identity which is its consummation.

Thus we see how God draws no being to Himself, communicates to none His own interiority, without arousing in him the movement which makes him no longer his own.

Thus it is established that we possess our self only in giving, that we are saved only by consenting to be lost, and that everywhere our being is measured by what we give.

This is the foundation of the necessity for redemption of that Poverty in spirit which is the first Beatitude. We know with what fervour St. Francis loved Poverty, which he called his Lady, and whose honour he defended with so jealous a zeal that in a friar minor the least shadow of possession seemed to him an outrage.

For its praise he found words of marvellous nobleness; and he never took his seat at the table of the rich unless Poverty was admitted with him under the figure of the bread he had received as alms.

Poverty he saw as inseparable from Christ; and if he wished it to be so absolute, it was because in a certain manner it was identical with God. And in truth if evangelical poverty consists above all in despoilment of self, in that interior dis-possession which yields up the whole being to God's good pleasure by in some sense transferring our Self into Him so that our soul becomes no more than a gaze of love directed to Him: can we not see in the subsistent altruism which constitutes the divine Persons—by making of each a living relation to the two others—the supreme exemplar and the eminent realisation of holy Poverty?

It is from this total disappropriation in the god-head that the infinite transparence flows which is in the Word the brightness of the eternal Light, the utter simplicity wherein is no shadow of change, the eternal infancy and the heart-rending innocence which were seen by Claudel at the vespers of Christmas at which he made the divine encounter.[1]

The Incarnation has its eternal repercussion in the humanity which subsists in God, which has its

[1] Dec. 25, 1886. Cf. Charles du Bos *Approximations*, 6ᵉ série, ed. Corrêa p. 287.

Self in the Word and which is the living parable of the eternal mind, the subsistent *élan* of the relations within the Trinity. And the movement is carried on into the Mystery of the church where everything is ordered to the putting off of the old man in the putting on of Christ, which finds in the very heart of the Liturgy its supreme expression:

> *This is My Body,*
> *This is My Blood.*

And does not the whole sacramental economy make of matter itself a reality purely relative to God who uses it for the communication to us of His grace?[1] And at the same time, by a mysterious correspondence, analogy obliges the words to grow immeasurably beyond themselves, to renounce their own being in order to strive toward the Ineffable while confessing their powerlessness to express what He is, carrying language to the point where in its very humility it becomes sheer transparence; while the priesthood in its turn strips the priests of their own self by identifying them with the Saviour who says "My" through their lips; so that ultimately,

[1] The symbolism incorporated in the Liturgy is closely related to the gift of Wisdom, since it leads us to see all things in the light of the one Face whose splendour shines upon the face of things, when matter, grown translucent to the regard of Faith, has entered into sublime poverty.

to the eye of faith, the Church is always and only *Jesus* in the translucent action of the signs, living or not, which in some manner represent Him and give Him to us.

And what is true of the sacraments which affect the interior life is not less true of the life itself.

All the mystical theology which leads the soul to the spiritual marriage by the crucifying betrothal of the Nights tends only to this disappropriation, the pure altruism which makes of the divine life—now become its own—the sole source and the sole rule of all its activity. Under the force of the transforming union which makes it gravitate toward God, the soul consummated in Charity now reacts only to His attraction and is sensible only of His light.

It has so full a sense of the divine glory that it instinctively judges of everything by relation to it, guided by the perfection of touch which results from the supreme interiority of a love entirely stripped of self, by the infallible taste for the savour of God which precisely *is* the gift of Wisdom, as the loveliest flower in the unseen diadem of most holy Poverty.

If Poverty is of this amplitude, if it can give us the most moving synthesis of the Christian faith, then obviously it must be a most powerful key to the Mystery of Mary, which can be stated in one phrase as a living relation to the Word made flesh.

In her, assuredly, more than in any other creature, Wisdom and Poverty are identified in the ceaseless oblation of her whole being by which she stands for ever as a monstrance for the showing forth of her Son.

I have tried to show how Wisdom and Poverty met in her marriage to Joseph and in her maternity, in her silence and her compassion, in our worship of her and in the dogmas which tell of her life in the Church. The constant source of her greatness is in the total altruism of her being and her life, and if she is the Seat of Wisdom *par excellence* it is because she is in a unique sense the Woman who was Poor, who entered deeper than any other soul into the abyss of the first Beatitude in which is contained all the joy of the gospel:

Blessed are the poor in spirit for theirs is the Kingdom of Heaven. (Matt. v. 3)